The Civilian Life Field Manual

How to Adjust to the Civilian World after Military Service

Jeremy P. Crosby, Psy.D.

You have permission to print, email, post, share, and pass along the digital version of *The Civilian Life Field Manual*, as long as no changes or edits are made to the contents or to the digital format.

Please share this with military veterans, their families, mental health professionals, medical treatment providers, and any person interested in helping veterans. However, the right to bind and sell it as a book is strictly prohibited.

The information in this book is not intended to be considered legal, medical, or any other professional service. The use of this book, or the information contained herein, does not constitute a professional, therapeutic, or other relationship with the author, and is not a substitute for professional care or mental health treatment. If you need or desire legal, medical, mental health, or other professional assistance, please consult with a competent professional. The author is not liable for any consequences arising from the use of this book or the information contained herein.

© 2010 Jeremy P. Crosby

Published by
Dog Ear Publishing
4010 W. 86th Street, Ste H
Indianapolis, IN 46268
www.dogearpublishing.net

ISBN: 978-160844-844-9

This book is printed on acid-free paper.

සි

This book is dedicated to all persons who have served in the military and wish to continue their service and contribution on the civilian side with honor, integrity, and a healthy adjustment.

Contents

Foreword

Introduction

Bibliography

Foreword

As veterans, we are everyday people. However, we have also been through unimaginable experiences that we hope most people never have to go through. We were well trained for our duties, but our minds could never be completely prepared for what we did and saw on the battlefield. Due to the impact of our experiences, retraining our hearts and souls for life in the "world" was needed.

When I came back from the Vietnam War missing two legs and my right arm, I wanted to be useful in the civilian world. I concentrated on public service in the political arena. I find that regardless of their background, all veterans want to continue to serve and contribute to this country and be useful. However, we must adjust to this world as we find it.

Guidance for this readjustment has been largely absent for past generations of veterans. They have largely been left to fend for themselves when it came to reentering civilian life in terms of personal readjustment. Recently, the effects of war and its impact on the mind and soul, has come under greater notice. From experience, I know that physical and emotional recovery from war is difficult, yet possible.

Dr. Crosby's book provides brilliant and common-sense insight as to how to use our military experience to do more than survive in this world. We can learn to thrive! I wish that for you in every way.

Max Cleland
Former U.S. Senator
Atlanta, Georgia
September 2010

Introduction

Welcome to ***The Civilian Life Field Manual***. This small book is a guide for navigating the often confusing terrain of civilian life after military service.

The rules of appropriate and successful conduct are different from what you have operated under in military culture. You will need to develop a new set of behaviors and skills for a healthy adjustment. This will take some dedication and work, but the benefits are enormous for you and your family.

A healthy and successful adjustment to civilian life is possible. What you do from this point forward in your life is your choice and your responsibility. However, with some key knowledge and guidance, the transition can go much better than it has for many veterans in years past.

The intent of this Field Manual is to provide information that supports veterans on the path toward a healthy and successful readjustment to civilian life after military service. There is also a companion audio program titled Military PDY (i.e., post-duty years) that is available as an additional readjustment resource at http://drjeremycrosby.com.

Following each chapter is a "notes page." To get the best benefit from what you find in the pages that follow, think of how each key point applies in your life today, jot some notes, and refer to them as you continue applying the principles for a healthy readjustment to your daily life.

For problems or symptoms beyond the scope of this book, please see Appendix D and consult with your physician or a licensed mental health provider.

I wish for you the best as you move into this new and hopefully good chapter of your life.

-Jeremy P. Crosby

Chapter 1   Welcome Home

If no one has said it yet, Welcome Home!

<u>Thank you</u> for your service.

Many veterans have expressed the frustration of not having been given debriefing, de-programming, or instruction for how to readjust and succeed in civilian life after their military service. Your chances of a healthy and successful adjustment will increase dramatically by implementing the principles and new skills described in this book.

<u>Key Point #1</u>: Most people in the civilian world don't know what you've done or why, <u>but you do</u>.

Don't expect people to understand something for which they have no background, training, or frame of reference.

For many veterans, your military career has been the most influential set of experiences that have shaped you and your life. However, it is not the entirety of your life.

<u>Key Point #2</u>: You are no longer on duty.

It is important to now give yourself permission to relax, enjoy life, and invest your time and energy into family, career, and your community. Continuing to live as if you were still on duty creates a "military mode of operating" that is counterproductive to a healthy adjustment in the civilian world.

You will not forget your military training and skills. However, it is now time to build additional perspectives and skills that match the realities of civilian life.

<u>Key Point #3</u>: Don't expect to pick up right where you left off when you joined the military.

Having some ideas for what to expect in adjusting to the civilian world will increase your chances for success. Generations of warriors have made this transition before you, and you won't be the last. A successful transition is possible!

The world has changed and it's a different life now. In the military, success is achieved by following orders and conforming to rules, regulations, and regimentation. To succeed in civilian life, the formula is <u>very different</u>.

<u>Key Point #4</u>: Now, it is up to you to create your own life.

<u>Now, the basic rules are</u>:

1. Don't hurt other people.

2. Follow most of the rules most of the time.

3. Generally get along with, or at least tolerate, most people.

The life that you create for yourself from this point forward will be of your own making. At first, this thought might cause some anxiety if you have been comfortable within the boundaries and direction that was provided by the military.

This can also be an <u>exciting</u> time based on new levels of freedom to choose and create the things you want in your career and in your life.

Just as with most issues you will encounter, there is no single perfect choice or life direction to be had. Many possible paths can be a good choice if they are consistent with your core values, and are good and beneficial to yourself, your family, your community, and to society.

<u>Key Point #5</u>: Many people who are coming out of the military already have many Positive Traits and Behaviors that are necessary for success (if utilized properly).

<u>Consider the following</u>:

- Loyalty
- Attention to detail
- Making sure that your work is "on purpose"
- Camaraderie
- Having high standards
- Conscientious
- Improvise, adapt, and overcome
- Determination
- Persistence
- Self-discipline
- Following regimentation and production schedules
- Courage
- Respect
- Integrity
- Commitment to overcoming challenges
- Getting a job done and done well!

Even with these traits and mindsets, there are still many sticking points that you need to know about.

In the following chapters, you will become familiar with the typical challenges and problems faced by veterans who are in the process of adjusting to civilian life. You will also be given the keys for how to overcome them.

We will visit each potential hurdle, and consider strategies and solutions for being aware, and for making the adjustments effectively.

<u>Notes</u>

_____

_____

_____

_____

_____

_____

_____

_____

_____

_____

_____

_____

_____

_____

_____

Chapter 2   What is Normal?

A basic psychological rule is that "normal" depends on the situation. This principle is a call to focus on taking <u>personal responsibility</u> for your <u>choices and actions</u> within the specifics of a given situation.

<u>Key Point #6</u>: The behaviors that have been "normal" in many military situations might not be "normal" in many civilian situations.

Your challenge is to learn new perspectives and behaviors that more accurately match the reality of the situations you encounter on a daily basis.

Realize that your beliefs are simply the result of conclusions you have accepted as being true for you, based on your training and past experience. To change your beliefs about a particular topic you must arrive at, and accept, new conclusions. [Please read the above sentence again. It is a powerful step for making positive change and regaining healthy control in your life.]

<u>Something to Think About</u>:

1. What is normal for a person, who has <u>never</u> been in the military, never had a trauma or potentially life-threatening experience, never was trained with intense and persistent discipline, and has never struggled for much of anything in their life?

2. What is normal for a person who has been intensely trained in combat and related missions, has used a variety of weapons, has practiced a range of survival

skills, has some medical knowledge to help injured or wounded buddies, and had this training reinforced in the most intense of environments known as "war"?

Is it a realistic expectation that the first person is going to fully understand what the second person experienced in a combat zone?

No way.

Is the second person going to come home, get out of the military, and then just magically forget all of that training and personal experience?

Not a chance.

Instead of forgetting, the goal is to <u>build on</u> the knowledge and skills that served you very well while you were in the military. To expand and continue our personal development makes us better in most every area of life.

One of the keys to success is making your behaviors <u>match the reality</u> of the situations you encounter.

<u>**Key Point #7**</u>: **You will need to develop new coping skills that match the reality of daily situations in civilian life.**

A <u>coping skill</u> is any thought, behavior, strategy, or action that you use to deal with a stressful situation or problem that you encounter. They are also called life skills, strategies, techniques, or "mental tools."

We all develop various kinds of skills growing up and as a product of our training (at any age) – this is normal. Now, an expanded set of skills will be required for effectively dealing with daily civilian life situations.

Examples of healthy coping skills include: Deep breathing, taking a time out, thinking of options, setting healthy boundaries, and checking your perceptions.

A healthy adjustment to civilian life will require some <u>knowledge, awareness, and intentional effort</u> on your part. You probably already possess some (or even many) of the necessary skills. Now, it is a matter of expanding their use to a wider range of situations, and also learning some higher level skills.

You, your family, and society will benefit greatly from a successful readjustment in your post-duty years, but it will take attention and effort in learning and practicing your new (or expanded) skills.

The good news is that skills are learnable, and you have been through similar processes before.

Notes

_____

_____

_____

_____

_____

_____

_____

_____

_____

_____

_____

_____

_____

_____

Chapter 3   The Need for Structure

In the military, you had structure <u>built in for you</u> and there was Chain of Command. You did not have to put much thought into these things. You did what you were told.

<u>Key Point #8</u>: Now, you have to become self-structuring.

Remember that it's up to you to <u>create your own life</u>. You will now have to put forth some time and effort to plan and schedule your own time. You will need to sit down and write out goals that you have chosen for yourself for the next 1 to 3 to 5 years. You will need a monthly household budget.

No one is magically coming to the rescue, but <u>there is help available</u> if you need some and are willing to receive it and cooperate with it (see Appendix D).

Plans are great until first contact. As life develops over time, you will need to make regular adjustments to your plans, priorities, and structure. By doing this your chances of success increase dramatically.

If you don't develop and implement these self-structuring skills, the events of life will toss you to-and-fro, and your level of control over your own life will be slim-to-none.

With this awareness and effort, you can exercise a healthy level of control in your life.

<u>Key Point #9</u>: In some places in civilian life, it might seem that no one is really in charge.

Most people in the civilian world are doing their own thing, caught up in their own little world, trying to be as happy as possible.

In this state of affairs, you must look to yourself for structure, direction, and guidance. This does not mean there is no help, mentoring, or assistance available to you. Think for yourself, make your own plans for yourself and your family, and then seek out help when you need it.

In reality, we all will eventually need some kind of help with something. <u>If you refuse to accept help you are limiting yourself, and possibly your family</u>.

Also, be aware that in the working world, you won't always get the information you need from the higher levels of the business structure. At times, you will need to seek out information. At other times, you have to do the best you can with incomplete information.

<u>Key Point #10</u>: In the end, you must make your own choices for yourself.

One aspect of this key point that cannot be overemphasized is the conclusion that <u>most negative consequences are the result of poor choices</u>. Better decision making tends to produce better circumstances for your life.

Be aware of this, and you can avoid many mistakes and lost time trying to figure things out the hard way.

The sooner a person gets beyond the tendency to blame other people and situations for undesirable outcomes, the sooner it becomes possible to take charge of one's own life and get more positive results.

Life is a series of choices that have corresponding outcomes. As you make better and better choices, the results in your life tend to improve in a corresponding way.

Do you accept that this is reality?   YES   NO

What decisions or choices are you making during this time period in your life?

What will be the long term implications?

Notes

Chapter 4   Strategic and Tactical

Think about the big picture of how the military gets things done.

A Mission is decided upon.

Next, we have 3 levels:
1. Strategic Plans
2. Tactical Implementation
3. The After Action Report and Evaluation.

When done well, this approach is a model for success.

Here is the reality of your current situation:

Key Point #11: You now have to be both the commander _and_ the enlisted person.

It is up to you to set your own goals, develop strategies, make your own decisions, and then carry them out. No one is coming to the rescue for what you decide or for the actions you choose to take.

To succeed, you need to do well in both roles. Again, there is help available if you choose to access it.

Key Point #12: To succeed, you must become empowered to direct your own life through good choices.

Let's consider how the military model can be used to increase the levels of freedom and control you have in your life, by applying good choices.

<u>The Military Model applied in Civilian Life</u>:

Your **Mission** = goals for yourself and your family.

Strategy = <u>Carefully thought-out plans for how to reach your goals</u>. Examples include decisions for where to live, how to earn an income, use of a budget, and other *planning*.

Tactics = <u>Actions and methods that "make it happen."</u> This includes things like your daily and weekly schedule, healthy habits, positive productive rituals, and day-to-day *actions you take* to accomplish tasks and move toward desired outcomes.

After Action Report = <u>An evaluation of how your strategy and tactics are working</u>. At least once per week look at your written goals, budget, schedule, and patterns of behavior.
- What is working?
- What needs to be changed (or at least modified)?
- Now, make changes accordingly.

<u>Key Point #13</u>: The best decisions are real-time decisions that are consistent with your strategy.

Life happens right now in the moment-to-moment experiences of your day. For decisions to be good decisions, they need to be based on current and accurate information, and need to match the reality of the situation.

When decisions are made in this way using the military model, chances for success increase rapidly.

If you get this basic model in your mind, you will be ahead of most people trying to make it in the civilian world, no matter what industry you work in.

- Mission
- Strategy
- Tactical Implementation
- After Action Report and Evaluation

Don't get caught up in everything that seems inefficient in the world. Instead, focus on growing and improving **yourself**, and <u>using **your** strengths</u> to contribute to **your** family, **your** community, and the world.

Notes

_____

_____

_____

_____

_____

_____

_____

_____

_____

_____

_____

_____

_____

_____

Chapter 5   Understanding Civilian People

Remember how a military operation works? You pull together with your Comrades and do whatever it takes for the mission to succeed. You take care of your people and put your own wants and needs dead last. You are also willing to suffer for the sake of the mission and caring for your people.

In civilian life, most veterans tend to operate in the same way. Let me repeat. In civilian life, most veterans tend to operate in the same way that worked for them in the military. Trouble occurs because those old solutions often <u>do not match</u> the reality of current situations.

If you don't make the transition to operating effectively on the civilian side of things, you will tend to wind up <u>very productive</u> at your work, but make <u>little to no progress</u> in your personal life. You will find that you are now stagnant, in a holding pattern, and feel stunted. You work harder and care more than anyone, but your life is on hold or in limbo. You are going through the paces but not getting anywhere – just treading water and working extremely hard at it.

<u>Key Point #14</u>: You will find a very <u>wide range</u> of motivation and abilities among the people in the civilian world.

It can be easy to conclude that people who aren't as Gung Ho! as you, or don't work as hard as you, must be lazy.

Most people <u>have not</u> had the training or experience that it takes to be extremely disciplined and persistent. Many people have a mindset that is geared for 9 to 5, and are not thinking about <u>keeping at something</u> until the job is done, and done well.

It's a fact – some people do just enough to "get by." But, don't fall into the trap of thinking that most people are that way. In reality, there are wide ranging levels of ability and motivation, and everyone has challenges in their life that you don't know about.

Learn to accept that not everyone can or will do an excellent or outstanding job. Expecting everyone to perform at an exceptional level is a setup for frustration and disappointment.

<u>**Key Point #15**</u>: **Barking orders and making strong demands does not work very well in civilian life.**

Be careful not to push people too hard in the civilian working world. Most people don't respond well to having orders barked at them or high-intensity approaches for motivating them.

In civilian life, most people see anger as inappropriate and frightening. With anger or intimidation, you might get some short-term initial results. However, many people will retaliate against these methods with passive or indirect behavior.

To get ahead of the game, teach yourself how to operate with skill and knowledgeable methods. Sometimes you need to be clever. Other situations will call for subtle actions or an indirect approach.

Most people don't know what you know, and don't have the military training and skills you have. They most likely <u>will not</u> think or perform as you do.

Using your best thinking and strategy is usually more effective than trying to intimidate people or cramming your ideas down their throat.

Focus on increasing your understanding, and then your level of power and control will increase considerably.

<u>Key Point #16</u>: If you are in a leadership position, figure out what motivates each person, and then strive to reward their performance in that way.

It's still true – you will catch more flies with sugar than vinegar.

You might find it difficult to identify with people who have lived on the civilian side of things their whole lives. However, some skill in dealing with people this way pays big dividends.

<u>Do</u> the following:

- Take a friendly approach
- Use tact
- Listen
- Try to understand their point of view
- Let other people take credit
- Identify the other person's positive qualities
- If you must disagree, do it in an agreeable way
- Make situations a win-win if at all possible

<u>Don't</u>:

- Take on every possible argument or challenge
- Go around telling people that they are wrong, stupid, or incompetent
- Criticize or embarrass people
- Micromanage (it kills morale quickly)
- Demand the impossible
- Exert your power just because you can
- Try to <u>force</u> things to happen

<u>Key Point #17</u>: You will most likely need to (at least occasionally) socialize with veterans in order to feel understood.

The overall tone of your social group will influence you more than you realize.

Make sure to find a group that is positive and avoid those who are intent on complaining or focusing on some type of negativity. Make sure to associate with people who are supportive of your forward positive progress in life.

In general, it is usually best to avoid people and groups who only want to complain or cast themselves in a victim role.

Notes

_____

_____

_____

_____

_____

_____

_____

_____

_____

_____

_____

_____

_____

_____

Chapter 6   Rules vs. Guidelines

Why have so many veterans through the years struggled with readjustment to civilian life?

Without new training, most people take the knowledge and skills they have and apply them in most every situation they encounter. The conflict arises when most situations in civilian life require a different set of behaviors and solutions than what was acceptable or useful in the military (especially in a war zone).

<u>Key Point #18</u>: Many areas of civilian life don't have clear cut rules, SOP's, a training manual, or definite answers and solutions.

Many veterans have a tendency to perceive situations as having strict rules due to their experience with the structure and methods of the military. It can be easy to have no tolerance for people who tend to see most rules, directives, and mandates more as guidelines.

What if at the store, the person in front of you has 23 items in the "20 items or less" line, and in your thinking is clearly out of compliance? <u>It is not your role</u> to "enforce the rules" or "teach them a lesson."

Successful adjustment requires being flexible in these kinds of situations that <u>are of low importance</u>.

What does **Improvise – Adapt – Overcome** mean in a civilian context?

Try to be cooperative, patient, and thoughtful in order to get things done.

In the military, some changes must happen quickly because of the life-and-death nature of the situations. However, in many civilian situations that <u>are not</u> life threatening, changes tend to be fairly slow. It takes time to develop and implement solutions that are well-thought-out, prudent, and effective.

Not everything is cut-and-dried or black-and-white. You will encounter many gray areas. Insisting that there are no gray areas will cause you grief, and provide very little practical benefit.

<u>Key Point #19</u>: You need to <u>not</u> take on every potential battle or challenge that comes your way.

In the military, leadership decides which battles to fight. Now, <u>you</u> must decide because it is <u>your</u> life. And remember, what you choose will also affect your family.

Nobody wins them all – that's just reality.

Only take on situations or challenges that are <u>actually worth</u> your time and effort.

Ask yourself: "What is to be gained?" _____

Then ask yourself, "Really?" _____

<u>Key Point #20</u>: Redefine in your mind, what is a big deal <u>vs.</u> what is a minor detail.

Historically, many veterans tend to continue using the mission-oriented mindset and apply it to most every detail of every situation, regardless of the facts of the situation.

The tendency is to overestimate the importance and intensity of most situations, resulting in overreactions.

<u>Begin to see situations as</u>:

- Low

- Medium

- High

- intensity, and then choose behaviors that match the reality of the situation.

<u>Hint</u>: If it is <u>not</u> immediately life-and-death, then it is most likely in the Medium to Low intensity range.

<u>Key Point #21</u>: Seriously consider changing the terminology you use.

If you use the word "battle" as in "choose your battles," then everything is viewed as a fight. Replace this with words like challenge or situation.

Your mindset will be much more effective by doing this.

Also, replace the word "<u>mission</u>" with terms like <u>objectives</u> or <u>goals</u>. For a minor situation, call it a task.

For example: Changing a light bulb is not a mission. It is just a small task that you do, and then move on.

This brings the intensity at which you operate down to a level that more closely matches the reality of the situation.

Key Point #22: Make finding cooperative and peaceful solutions a primary goal.

Clearly, military training teaches you to react to threatening situations, attack the opposition, and win by overpowering and overwhelming your opponent.

It takes some awareness and intentional effort to move away from this mode of operating and to seek peaceful solutions for most situations (and/or conflicts).

Being aware of this puts you several steps ahead of most veterans who found this out through the school of hard knocks.

Using <u>new solutions</u> that work in your current situation is the key to adjusting well and succeeding in this chapter of your life.

Most situations really do have peaceful solutions. To achieve them we need to be willing to cooperate with others, and be mindful of operating this way.

<u>Notes</u>

Chapter 7   Responding vs. Reacting

Many veterans tend to live in "reaction mode" much of the time as a result of intense military training and/or experiences in a combat zone. This behavior helped you to be successful in the military, and most likely helped you stay alive.

However, when <u>reacting</u> in civilian life, we don't think, and that can cause much trouble in current situations.

<u>Notice the difference</u>:

React – taking immediate action without thinking.

Respond – taking action based on thinking; having well-thought-out reasons for what you will do, and why.

<u>**Key Point # 23**</u>: **When you <u>react</u> in routine daily situations, you give your control away.**

To cope more effectively, we want to maintain our self-control. This is crucial to success in most things.

When a stressful situation arises, first STOP!
(Notice that it's not life-and-death, just stressful.)

Now, focus on your thinking.

Say to yourself, "<u>What are my options</u>?"

Look for the most appropriate way of handling this situation or event.

After you have <u>thought it through</u>, take action on the most reasonable and rational option.

Once you get some practice in operating this way, it only takes 10 to 30 seconds in most routine daily situations to think of reasonable and effective solutions or answers.

With continued practice, you will find yourself handling situations better than you have in the past and getting fewer negative consequences from your behavior.

Please take this technique seriously. The benefits of <u>Responding</u>, and Not Reacting, are huge.

By actually slowing down, you are now considering more information, sorting and evaluating the information, seeing the likely consequences of potential courses of action, and making more informed and higher quality decisions.

We see that faster is not always better – especially when it comes to making important decisions and using good judgment.

<u>Remember the key steps</u>:
1.   STOP
2.   THINK
3.   CHOOSE (a good option)
4.   <u>Now</u>, RESPOND (with good coping)

Notes

_____

_____

_____

_____

_____

_____

_____

_____

_____

_____

_____

_____

_____

_____

Chapter 8   Dealing with Frustrations

Key Point #24: **Having extremely high expectations of other people will cause you problems.**

You are most likely used to a high performance mindset and corresponding behaviors. Remember that other people don't know what you know, haven't seen what you've seen, and don't have the training you have. Expecting them to think and perform in the high performance ways that you are used to is a setup for disappointment, frustration, and anger.

People can perform only to the level of their current awareness and training. Most people will do what they were trained to do.

Key Point #25: **Modifying your style of communication can prevent many problems and misunderstandings.**

In the civilian world, it is expected that you will be assertive, but also tactful and cooperative.

In the military, the norm is to speak up, be heard, and speak a little louder to <u>make sure</u> that you were heard.

This very direct style, paired with more volume <u>than is common</u> in most civilian situations, often comes off as harsh, rude, socially rough, and yelling (when you actually intended none of that). Your only intention was to be clear and be heard – that's it.

Careful and intentional use of your words with less volume in your voice can be helpful.

<u>Key Point #26</u>: Be willing to hear and consider feedback from others.

In communication, listening is the most important skill you can develop. The best listener is usually the most informed and most powerful person in the room.

Most people want to speak, be heard, and feel important. As a result, really good listening is rare among most individuals and groups of people. Careful listening can often reduce your frustrations by providing necessary information or answers.

<u>Key Point #27</u>: Many people in leadership positions will have limited leadership skills.

There is no magic cure for this, as it is a common complaint in many organizations.

You might need to own your own business, or be willing to allow those in leadership positions to implement some of your ideas.

If you are forceful or aggressive in trying to fix this where you work, you will usually get the opposite of what you really want.

Also, be aware that there are several legitimate leadership styles. Different styles or approaches are often needed depending upon specifics of a situation or the abilities of the people involved.

Don't fall into the trap of thinking that there is only one effective approach to leadership.

<u>**Key Point #28**</u>: **Many organizations seem to lack structure, logical organization, SOP's, chain of command, or clear processes and procedures.**

This situation might be an opportunity for you to work your way into a position where you can make valuable contributions.

If the chaos seems beyond repair, it might be your signal to move on to a more workable environment.

Make sure to give yourself enough time to use good judgment and make a good decision. Some of these situations are fixable, but others will seem to be impossible. Sometimes, if a situation is beyond repair, the best thing to do is just move on.

You will adjust much faster when you accept that people are the way they are.

Choose to focus your energies on things that can be changed. Don't waste your energy on the rest.

Notes

_____

_____

_____

_____

_____

_____

_____

_____

_____

_____

_____

_____

_____

_____

Chapter 9   Building on Strengths

Key Point #29: **You most likely already have many traits that are needed for success.**

These traits include being willing to put forth effort, knowing the things you intend to accomplish, persistence, a success mindset that says "failure is not an option," determination, self-discipline, courage, and the pursuit of excellence in your work.

Skills for dealing with people include:

- Flexibility in the midst of a project
- Composure
- Working as a team
- Don't take things personally
- Let other people save face
- Compassion for the weak
- Strive for fairness and equity
- Give credit where credit is due

Thinking skills that lead to success include:

- Define a problem at the root level
- Be specific about your goals
- Seek out information
- Assess situations thoroughly
- Think ahead (make strategies and plans)
- Continually compare results to the standards of performance
- Use new information to adjust to changing times, standards, or trends

<u>Additional strengths to draw upon include</u>:

- Valuing friends and family
- Being protective of your people
- Usually being alert and aware
- Always being prepared
- Not taking things for granted
- Being trustworthy and responsible
- Dedicated and hard working
- Having high standards
- Conscientious
- Caring about the greater good
- Having a sense of honor
- Wanting to work, be productive, and contribute to good results and outcomes
- A clever sense of humor

Go back and put a check beside those strengths you recognized in yourself?

Most employers want this kind of person to work for them. A healthy adjustment to civilian life requires that you become aware of these traits and implement them with awareness in your daily life.

<u>Key Point #30</u>: A traditional job may or may not be best for you.

You might need to work alone, have a large amount of control over your work, work for yourself, own your own business, utilize accommodations for any physical injuries, and/or have a flexible work schedule to accommodate medical appointments.

Understanding some basics of your own personality can provide direction for choosing the types of work that are most suitable to your unique personality traits.

For a personalized set of ideas about work and career, you can take the Keirsey Temperament Sorter. It is available for an affordable price at www.keirsey.com.

Request the following reports:

[1]Career Temperament Report

[2]Learning Styles Temperament Report

Consider this a cost-effective way to save time and make more informed decisions to get headed in a well-chosen direction for your career and your future.

Notes

_____

_____

_____

_____

_____

_____

_____

_____

_____

_____

_____

_____

_____

_____

_____

Chapter 10   New Meanings

In the world of psychology, many professionals agree that for things to change in a positive direction, you must change your thoughts.

Key Point #31: To make positive changes in your life, you will need to change your thinking.

By expanding your perspective and refining your understanding of key issues, you can avoid the traps of lingering old thought patterns. These old viewpoints worked for you in the high-intensity situations of the past, but will be out of context and most likely unproductive in the new situations of your life.

Consider the following six ideas:

1.   Ambush
The military teaches you to Achieve fire superiority as quickly as possible! This approach in civilian life will just push people away or create resistance against you. If a situation is not life-threatening right at this moment, then pause, think, and respond based on good thinking and problem solving.

Surprising situations no longer have to represent an ambush or attack upon you. Instead, you can stop, think, figure it out, and then proceed without resorting to overpowering force, or bludgeoning people.

2. Improvise, Adapt, and Overcome

The Old Way of operating involves using whatever is at hand and eliminating the enemy with vicious intensity. In civilian life, the key to success is to use your thinking skills to find the best solution for the situation or problem.

Stop trying to overpower everyone and every situation you encounter. Be flexible, solve the problem with a cooperative or win-win approach, and make it work.

3. Competitiveness

The military teaches a level of intensity that few people (other than hard core athletes) understand. To adjust in the civilian world, it is important to stop turning every little situation into an all-out, high intensity competition.

There really are events that are not about winning. Many situations in the civilian world are about participation and connecting with other people. With practice you can tell the difference between events that are serious competition, and events that are more social and cooperative in nature.

4. Perfectionism

Combat training (and experience) teaches you to do everything perfectly the first time, or you and your buddies could die. This quickly instills the attitude that absolutely no mistakes are allowed. This approach is not realistic in most civilian situations.

Instead, choose your standard to be <u>Excellence, not perfection</u>. Decide that <u>achieving excellence</u> is a fantastic outcome and you can live with that.

5. Trust
Many military experiences teach you that you can only trust people who've had the same training as you, or only those people "on your team." To function outside of a military context, it is critical to expand your view of trust beyond the all-or-nothing level, based on life-and-death scenarios.

Learning to exercise <u>partial trust</u> is necessary and functional in civilian life. We need to learn to trust some people for a few specific things, and only in specific situations. You will most likely get better and better at exercising good judgment in this. Instead of all-or-nothing trust, learn to trust people in the ways and to the extent that they prove trustworthy.

6. Honor
Honor is integrity plus doing something because it's the right thing. Most military veterans tend to identify with the belief that says: <u>do the right things for the right reasons</u>.

In civilian life, we can't always insist on other people using our methods. Keep your sense of honor based on doing the right things for the right reasons. However, accept that there are many methods that can get the excellent outcomes you desire without compromising your integrity.

Most of the time, we <u>don't</u> need to control the methods by which things get accomplished.

Notes

_____

_____

_____

_____

_____

_____

_____

_____

_____

_____

_____

_____

_____

_____

_____

Chapter 11   Potential Problems to Avoid

What happens if you don't adjust well to the Post-Duty Years?

Key Point #32: Certain problems are expectable if you don't adjust well during your post-duty years.

These potential problems include the following:
- Numerous jobs
- Relationship problems/Divorces
- A victim mindset
- Anger problems
- Perfectionism
- All-or-nothing mindsets (and actions)
- Overly high intensity and urgency
- Self-medicating with alcohol or drugs
- A low self-esteem

Please take note: If you start to self-medicate with alcohol or other drugs, this is a sign of some underlying problems or symptoms, and a warning to seek some treatment before things get out of control.

Key Point #33: You need to find ways to have excitement and enjoyment in your life, without your behavior being dominated by adrenaline and dangerousness.

It is completely normal to want some excitement, positive anticipation, and enjoyment in your life.

Civilian life will most likely seem very boring or slow paced compared to the high intensity and life-and-death nature of many past experiences in the military. Your challenge is to experience good enjoyment in life without having to live on the edge, or put yourself and others in danger.

By finding some exciting or fun things balanced with responsibility, life can be enjoyable.

Key Point #34: **You will need a long term plan.**

You must get beyond just a short term view, and develop goals for yourself and your career. You will need new ways to motivate yourself that do not involve anger or alcohol. These short term motivators usually bring unwanted side effects.

Perfectionism in civilian life creates unattainable standards leading to frustration and disappointments. Strive to do your best and be willing to keep modifying things along the way. That's just how it works in most situations you will encounter.

Key Point #35: **Rigid thinking will cause you problems.**

Be aware that all-or-nothing mindsets allow for no gray areas or flexibility. Most civilian life situations involve preferences and a wide range of acceptable (or even good) options.

Rigid thinking is based on exclusive views of "right vs. wrong" and defines situations in ways that do not fit reality or practicality. If some action is clearly wrong or unethical, then please stick with your beliefs and values for what constitutes good and right behavior.

However, when situations are not moral or ethical in nature, they usually require choices based on good judgment, assessment of the facts, or simply preferences.

Insisting that every action is either "right or wrong," does not fit with reality.

<u>Key Point #36</u>: You will need to practice flexibility, but without compromising your values, ethics, or honor.

High intensity and urgency create stress and anxiety in situations that do not call for such strong emotions or reactions.

If you need to swat a fly, don't reach for a bazooka. Realize that your training tells you to overwhelm the opposition. In the civilian world, this is overkill and most of the time unnecessary (including the mess).

Strive to exert the least amount of force that gets the job done. You will save a lot of energy and get much less mess in the process. Learn to operate in a cooperative way when possible, and focus on your strengths and the results you can produce.

<u>Key Point #37</u>: Certain thoughts and attitudes will limit you and your progress more than anything else.

<u>Here are several examples</u>:
- Feeling unappreciated.
- Staying angry at those people who don't seem to understand you and your methods.

- Insisting that your way is the right way and the only way.
- Festering with frustration and agitation at those people who don't do things your way.
- Refusing to listen to others' perspectives, or receive feedback about anything.
- Frequently perceiving situations as a "slap in the face" when you are not recognized in a positive way, or in the way that you would have liked.
- Feeling fully justified in harboring resentments and holding tightly to grudges.
- Indulging in contempt for other people's lack of awareness of the bigger issues of life.
- Focusing on negativity or your perceptions of how people fall short of your expectations.
- Believing that you must have control when it is not possible.

Make sure to give yourself credit for the things you do accomplish. Stay focused on making the best choices you can. Avoid the limiting mindsets by staying intent on the positive things that are possible.

Poor choices are usually at the root of most serious problems. A focus on what is possible, striving to improve your thinking and methods, and disciplined effort to make better choices can change most situations for the better.

Make an effort every day to stay aware, use better thinking skills, and make better choices based on good information and options.

<u>Consider the following corrective thoughts and attitudes:</u>

- I no longer need outside approval for doing the right things.
- Other people who have not had similar experiences probably won't understand, and that's O.K.
- There are many ways to get excellent results.
- I choose to listen and understand things first – this is critical to success in most endeavors.
- Lack of recognition is usually due to an oversight or unawareness. I refuse to take it personally.
- I choose to release past resentments so that I can heal and move forward to better things.
- We all have areas of life in need of growth and improved awareness.
- Most people are doing the best they can based on their past training and current level of awareness. Being angry at people or situations does not help them or improve things.
- I choose to exert the least amount of control that is needed to be responsible and get the job done well.

Notes

Chapter 12   Readjustment and Your Family

Key Point # 38: **Readjusting during your Post-Duty Years is not something best done alone.**

You need to talk with your spouse, significant other, and family members. It is critical to have an open mind and be willing to receive and consider feedback from family, friends, and loved ones. While they may not understand everything you have gone through, they are often your best source of feedback about your patterns of behavior.

Problems usually arise from a lack of understanding, not participating in the "normal activities" of kids and the family, missing out on parts of their lives, refusing to get close to family members emotionally, and keeping things bottled up.

Some veterans will be affected by symptoms such as anxiety, depression, or PTSD. If so, then help will be needed that exceeds the scope of this small book. That help is available and includes possible medication, talk therapy, and peer support, but you will have to seek it out if you are struggling.

Please see Appendix D and consult with your physician or a licensed mental health professional.

Thousands of veterans have worked through these symptoms and achieved a good and enjoyable life once again. If you keep everything secret, it will eat you up.

Key Point #39: DO NOT talk about the gory details of your military experiences with family members.

Sharing details of gory or traumatic events with family members is very unlikely to be beneficial. Possible emotional harm can result from sharing too much about the gory details of your experiences. When you talk with family and friends about your experiences, it is best to keep the information more general, or focus on positive and/or humorous events.

Seek out a professional who understands how to deal with extreme experiences, and can guide you in processing those experiences. Usually, traumatic experiences need to be processed in the safe environment of a one-to-one therapeutic relationship with a licensed therapist who specializes in treating trauma-related conditions.

Key Point #40: You will need to learn to feel again, and be willing to connect emotionally with loved ones.

It is very common to shut down or block off your emotions when in a combat zone or high intensity situations. This is necessary in order to stay focused and do your job.

The bond that keeps people in relationships and makes social connections work is emotional. To generally get along and be able to connect with others will require that you relearn to experience and connect with certain emotions.

Make sure to take "baby steps" as you begin to experience a wider range of feelings again. Proceeding too quickly usually causes people to become overwhelmed.

Key Point #41: If you have been deployed, relationships will require some adjustments.

No matter how good your family relationships have been in the past, time keeps moving forward and things change. Don't expect that relationships will simply pick up right where they left off.

With some willingness and effort, relationships can continue to be good. They can often be mended if that is what's needed and both parties are willing to put some effort toward rebuilding.

Key Point #42: If you are a family member, there are some things you can do to help your loved one.

- <u>Give Space</u>

   Notice symptoms or reactions and back off. Have a plan ahead of time. Use a code word so you both know what's going on and what behavior to expect from the other person.

- <u>Listen</u>

Don't try to fix it for them. Take the attitude "I'm always here for you if you do want to talk about it." If they don't want to talk about it, then accept that it's too painful right now and they might need more time or possibly some professional counseling.

- <u>Don't push for information about traumatic experiences</u>

This is seen as intrusive and unsafe. Respect your loved one's choice to not talk about things that were overwhelming, horrific, or even "unspeakable." Encourage them to seek professional therapy if overwhelmed or having severe symptoms.

- <u>Try to understand</u>

As a spouse, partner, or family member, learn as much as possible about what your loved one is going through. Realize that your understanding of their experience will always be incomplete. Don't say that you understand if you don't. Express that you want the best for them and are supportive.

- <u>Accept the person for who they are</u>

Focus on your loved one's positive strengths. Realize that if they get overwhelmed, they are trying their best, and the best thing you can do is to try and understand and be supportive.

- <u>Stop blaming and being negative toward the person</u>

Blaming fixes nothing. In an effort to "make them better" you are pushing them away. Realize that the issue of rejection is already a hot button for many veterans who have had very intense experiences.

- <u>Accept that it's not your job to "fix them"</u>

Allow the person to find the answers they need. Encourage and support them, but don't push. Trying to force things usually makes things worse.

- <u>Be part of the recovery process – get therapy for yourself</u> (Options might include individual therapy, couples therapy, and/or family therapy.)

The most helpful thing is to work on any issues you might have and then be supportive. Learn what to do and what not to do. For example, to wake the person from sleep, never grab them, shake them, or yell. You will probably get hit (or worse). Learn to touch the person's foot and calmly call their first name to awaken them.

- <u>Learn what the person's triggers are</u>

Focus on being a partner and helping them to be aware. Agree on a plan for how to remind the person of their coping skills and positive options. Make it clear that you are not trying to control them, but do want to help if possible.

- <u>Focus on being accepting and forgiving</u>

There are certain processes of adjustment that only the veteran can do. Being judgmental and angry at them only impedes the process. In the end, forgiveness and acceptance are extremely powerful healing processes, and are some of the most valuable gifts you can give another person. If you want good things for your loved one, then accept and forgive them.

- <u>Encourage the person to join in normal activities</u>

With support and increasing practice, a person can gradually do more activities that are part of "normal" family and community life. This will take some time – don't pressure them or rush it. Gently express that you would like them to join you and the family as much as possible. Accept that they will only do this as much as they are able and only when they are ready.

Individuals who receive healthy support from friends and family tend to readjust more quickly. Providing acceptance and support is powerful medicine and an expression of your love for them.

Notes

Chapter 13   Things That Have Worked

Realize that you now live under a different set of rules. The general culture and norms of the civilian world are very different from the culture of the military. The behaviors that are most successful are also different and will have to be learned, developed, or improved upon with practice.

Key Point #43: You will need to learn self-care as a regular part of your routines to keep yourself in good shape mentally and physically.

On a mission, your own wants and needs ranked close to the bottom of the list of priorities. In your life today, if you are broken down, exhausted, and drained you will not be in any shape to help others, especially those people close to you that you care about deeply.

Assertiveness skills are usually most effective, instead of attacking or being angry. Stand up for yourself, ask for what you want or need, and be persistent but <u>not forceful</u>.

Learn how to relax, and then make it a regular practice. It is proper and good that you take time on a regular basis to relax and enjoy things. By doing so, life will be more enjoyable and you will also recharge yourself mentally and physically, resulting in even more effectiveness in your work.

Key Point #44: **Realize that therapy is an investment in learning and retraining yourself, and is <u>not</u> a sign of weakness or that you are broken.**

Getting individual or group therapy, attending stress management or anger management classes, or getting personal coaching is an intentional effort to get some assistance and to invest in your own development and your future. Don't broadcast it, but don't be ashamed of it either.

You would take care of your equipment so that it would work for you. You need to do the same for your most valuable asset – your mind.

Try to get along with most people most of the time. Don't bludgeon people just because you can.

Stay sober.

Live in the present.

Change your thinking toward the positive.

Expect to succeed, but don't force it. Do everything that is reasonable, persist, and follow up. Then, <u>allow</u> the success to happen. You deserve it and so do the people in your life who rely on you.

Get productive thoughts into your head frequently as you deal with the challenges of daily life situations. Make a few coping skills cards using 3X5 index cards. Carry the cards with you at all times and refer often to this list of coping skills. (You can copy these productive thoughts from Appendix B and add your own.)

Key Point #45: **In reality, everyone needs help with some things eventually.**

Get help if you need it. Part of normal life is friends and neighbors helping each other and looking out for each other, without having to keep score or feel obligated that you owe them a favor. If you are able to do something that you are responsible for, then do it. If a task requires more than just you, then get some assistance. Doing this is not some kind of weakness. It is just part of the new normal for your life.

Don't personalize things. Most things <u>are not</u> an attack on you personally. Step back, put the words or event in context, and then move forward toward your goals. Refuse to take it on – especially when it is their problem, not yours. Many things are not a big deal. Learn to let the little things go.

Key Point #46: **Having normal routines and schedules will provide a baseline of stability from which you can grow and succeed.**

Remember that we said you need to be self-structuring now. With healthy routines and schedules that you have developed and now follow, your skills can emerge and work for you.

Instead of keeping you stuck in a rut, healthy routines are a solid foundation from which you operate. They provide a stable home base for your daily behaviors from which to operate, grow, and succeed.

<u>Skills that will serve you include the following</u>:

- Patience
- Seek understanding first
- Get perspective
- Use of good judgment in gray areas and situations involving a choice or preference
- Practice maturity
- Accept yourself and others
- Have an open mindset
- Get real answers
- Get to the actual root of problems or situations
- Focus on listening
- Believe in yourself
- Use your best thinking skills
- Accept yourself for the person you are
- Try forgiveness of yourself and others

Remember that some skills might be new, some you might have, and others might need to be practiced more or expanded.

Notes

Chapter 14   Conclusions

Again – Welcome Home!

<u>Thank You</u> for your service.

You more than anyone know the contribution you have made, and the actual value it represents.

You deserve a "heads up" for how to successfully make this transition to civilian life.

Let your spouse, significant other, or family members read this *Field Manual* so they can better join with you and support you over the next several weeks, months, and years.

<u>Key Point #47</u>: To improve your life requires a personal decision.

When this decision is followed by action and persistence in developing yourself and adapting to the reality of the new situations in your life, you are on the path toward a productive and enjoyable life in the post-duty years.

What you decide for your future is your choice. With this awareness, you are now in a position to take control of your life and your future through the power of your choices and actions.

Key Point #48: **Study this book at minimum once or twice every week for at least a year.**

Discuss it with your significant other and family members. Tell your therapist, mentor, or personal coach about it. You will be many years (and probably decades) ahead of other veterans who don't apply themselves in an intentional way to a healthy readjustment. Doing this will benefit you, your family, and your community immensely.

Key Point #49: **You still have many challenging and hopefully exciting experiences ahead of you.**

Many veterans have expressed how civilian life was extremely boring in comparison to the adrenaline-filled life-and-death situations of combat. Life <u>can</u> be enjoyable and good.

On this side of things, your life will be the product of your decisions and what you make of your time in life. Expect good outcomes and make the best decisions that will take you to the places and experiences that will be best for you and your family.

Key Point #50: **I wish for you the very best, and so do many other people.**

There are many people who care deeply about veterans and wish the very best for you. Often people don't know what to say, and don't know how to express their gratitude and support.

Let us all say **Thank You!** and **Welcome Home**.

<u>Notes</u>

_____

_____

_____

_____

_____

_____

_____

_____

_____

_____

_____

_____

_____

_____

_____

Appendix A

Basic Healthy Coping Skills
(Adapted from *A Mind Frozen in Time*, Crosby 2008)

- Deep Breathing → calm the mind and body.

- Take a Time Out! from a stressful or frustrating situation. Come back and deal with it in a better frame of mind.

- Stop → Think → Choose → Now take action.

- Step back and see the big picture → now proceed with a better overall perspective.

- <u>Respond</u> with thinking (don't react).

- Count to 10, stay calm, and always remain in control of yourself.

- Think to yourself, "What are my <u>Options</u>?"

- Practice relaxing in a safe place every day.

- Consider consequences before acting. Is that outcome what you really want?

- Say "No" when you need to.

- Exercise your mind some every day through reading.

- Talk with a friend (or a counselor if needed).

- Carry your coping card in your pocket, purse, or wallet. Read it several times daily.

- Gather your thoughts before you speak.

- Change what you can and let the rest go.

- Do something enjoyable every single day.

- Laugh some every day.

- Listen to music that you enjoy.

- Enjoy the company of a pet.

- Learn something new every day.

- Go to an enjoyable place or event. Take time to get enough rest.

- Maintain your schedule and routines (with flexibility).

- Take all medications exactly as prescribed.

- Ask yourself, "What positive alternative exists here?"

- Read books that help you increase your mental and emotional maturity.

- Ask questions if you are unsure or confused.

- Get help when you need it.

- Gather information, think slowly and deliberately, and then make your best decision.

- Detach from your ego. You don't have to prove yourself.

- Check your perceptions. Ask yourself, "Am I seeing this clearly?" Check your ideas with someone who is a good sounding board.

Appendix B

Thoughts to put on Your Coping Cards
(Adapted from *Mind Click*, Crosby 2009)

- Does this approach support the things I value?

- Is this consistent with my values and beliefs?

- I have the authority to choose what is important in my own life.

- What is my logic based on? Does it compute?

- The basis for this idea is _____.

- This makes sense in comparison to _____.

- Issues I care about deeply are _____.

- The purpose of my work is to _____.

- **D**iagnose, consider **O**ptions, **G**o for it (do it)!

- <u>For more serious situations</u>:
  1. Clarify the problem
  2. Get the facts
  3. Analyze the information
  4. Consider possible solutions (think of options)
  5. Choose your best option
  6. Implement, evaluate, and start the process again

- What are the expectable consequences of this choice?

- Exactly whose expectations am I trying to fulfill?

- How do I expect others to act? _____

- Is this expectation realistic?   YES   NO

- What are the facts? _____

- Is the data current?

- What are my <u>best</u> sources of information?

- <u>Remember</u>: Information alone is useless until it is analyzed, interpreted, and then applied.

- In what situations is this solution applicable?

- What is the root issue? Spell it out.

- Most problems have several desirable or acceptable solutions. Some solutions are better than others.

- Is there an obvious common sense solution that is reasonable? What is it?

- What do I really want here?

- How can I make things better?

- Why would this be a wise course of action?

- How is my past training coloring my perceptions?

- What are my assumptions about this _____?

- Numerous resources are available to me. I just need to identify them and access them.

- Not every resource has to be personally owned for it to benefit me.

- How else should we define the problem?

- What am I <u>really</u> trying to accomplish?

Appendix C

New Beliefs and Behaviors

(That make adjusting to the Post-Duty Years smoother)

1. My efforts are an investment (not a sacrifice).

2. It is okay to take care of myself, and it is necessary for long term success.

3. I strive for Excellence (not perfection).

4. I am willing to accept help with some things. Nobody succeeds on their own efforts alone.

5. I believe that I deserve to succeed, be rewarded, and make progress for myself and my family.

6. The better I become, the more I can contribute.

7. Most people are not my enemy. Most people are in their own little world, largely unaware, and not focused on me.

8. In most civilian life situations, there is no one right, perfect, or correct decision. There are usually many options, and some are better than others.

9. I choose to continue growing by learning, modifying, upgrading, and improving myself.

10. I choose to feel good, perform well, and keep improving. If it is to be, it is up to me.

Appendix D

Resources

U.S. Department of Veterans Affairs
http://www.va.gov

Military One Source
http://www.militaryonesource.com

Iraq and Afghanistan Veterans of America
http://iava.org

Vet Centers
http://www.vetcenter.va.gov

Possible Internet Search Terms
(put into an internet search engine)

- Help for veterans

- Army, Navy, Air Force, or Marines

- Post deployment

- Military veterans

Bibliography

Canfield, J. *The Success Principles*. New York: HarperCollins. 2005.

Cantrell, B. and Dean, C. *Once a Warrior, Wired for Life*. Seattle, WA: WordSmith Books. 2007.

Crosby, J. *A Mind Frozen in Time*. Indianapolis: Dog Ear Publishing. 2008.

Crosby, J. *Mind Click*. Indianapolis: Dog Ear Publishing. 2009.

Davis M, Eshelman ER, and McKay M. *The relaxation & stress reduction workbook, 5th Ed*. New York: New Harbinger Publications. 2000.

Dean C. *Nam vet*. Winepress Publishing. 1999, 10th printing.

de Bono, E. *Six Thinking Hats*. New York: Little, Brown and Company. 1999.

DeRoo C and DeRoo C. *What's Right With Me*. Oakland, CA: New Harbinger. 2006.

Grossman D, Lt. Col. *On killing: the psychological cost of learning to kill in war and society*. New York: Bay Back Books Little, Brown and Company. 1995.

Hawkins, D. *Power vs. Force*. Carlsbad, CA: Hay House. 2002.

Matsakis A. *I can't get over it: a handbook for trauma survivors, 2nd ed*. New York: New Harbinger Publications, Inc. 1996.

McKay M and Rogers P. *The anger control workbook*. New York: New Harbinger Publications. 2000.

Potter-Efron R and Potter-Efron P. *Letting go of anger.* New York: New Harbinger Publications. 1995.

Ray, J.A. *The Science of Success.* Carlsbad, CA: Sunark Press. 2006.

Sapolsky RM. *Why zebras don't get ulcers: an updated guide to stress, stress related diseases, and coping.* 3rd ed.: New York: Holt paperbacks. 2004.

Schiraldi GR. *The self-esteem workbook.* New York: New Harbinger Publications. 2001.

Shay J. *Achilles in Vietnam.* New York: Touchstone. 1994.

Watzlawick P, Weakland JH, and Fisch R. *Change: principles of problem formation and problem resolution.* New York: W.W. Norton & Company. 1974.

LaVergne, TN USA
11 February 2011
216228LV00004B/11/P